First

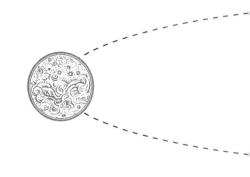

First

Arleen Paré

Brick Books

Library and Archives Canada Cataloguing in Publication

Title: First / Arleen Paré.
Names: Paré, Arleen, 1946– author.
Description: Poems.
Identifiers: Canadiana (print) 20200390899 | Canadiana (ebook) 20200390902 |
ISBN 9781771315425 (softcover) | ISBN 9781771315432 (HTML) |
ISBN 9781771315449 (PDF)
Classification: LCC PS8631.A7425 F57 2021 | DDC C811/.6—dc23

We gratefully acknowledge the Canada Council for the Arts, the Government of Canada
through the Canada Book Fund, and the Ontario Arts Council for their support of our
publishing program.

The author photo was taken by Chris Fox.
The book is set in Dante.
Designed by Marijke Friesen.
Printed and bound by Coach House Printing.

Brick Books
487 King St. W.
Kingston, ON
K7L 2X7
www.brickbooks.ca

For Pat Hurdle, my first best friend.

the radiance of first things
—Anne Simpson

Pat Hurdle and I met when she was six and I was five years old. We became best friends. When I was nine, I was made to change schools, Protestant to Catholic. This was the first interruption of our friendship, a terrible pall. Her mother died when she was fourteen, a second, worse pall. When I was eighteen, my family moved across town. Pat and I drifted, at first just a little, then a lot. I lost track of her. I was distracted; I got married. Had a husband, children, a career. I didn't really miss her. When I was thirty, my husband, kids, and I moved from Montreal to the West Coast. Later I fell in love, acquired a wife, and moved farther west to Victoria. At some point, I began to miss Pat a lot. I asked other childhood friends about her, but no one knew anything. Eventually I lost hope that I would ever see her again. And then five decades later, five decades after we had become best friends, her name appeared in my inbox, the subject line, Green Circle, *the street where we grew up. It turned out she'd been living on Vancouver Island, in Victoria, for several years, ten blocks from my house and three thousand miles from our childhood homes on Green Circle, Dorval. We'd landed in the same city, same neighbourhood, ten blocks apart, curving back on ourselves.*

Contents

Girls: The Green Time

The Curve of Time

Before the First, Before the Time

We don't know what this world
is, for it is never enough
and filled with infinite longing
—Len Anderson

It

... is simply   they say   cosmos and effect-
ive   cosmic tethers   laws of   theorems   bylaws

drill down   first light   slightly curved
which cause came before first   before laws

a casino's pale glow in the east
a Las Vegas desert   Orion's Arm

a bedroom window   a thought
furled as a fiddlehead fern
to begin

yes   no   the human mind
happy to meet you

Beginning in gravity

bless you   my dead twin   breathless companion
dying in our mother's womb
your back to the uterine wall
making room
the one who got away   vanishing
as if you were a mere syndrome
bless your striving
your ongoing friendliness
bless your giving up   foetus
papyrus   petals of white bougainvillea
starved or fated   struck with misfortune some hour of day
or night   in slow revolution   how
I still

carry you   how you carry me
missing
how much we are missing
bless your likeness   your lucent weight
eternal syncopation   your slow disintegration
continuous   your courage   mine

It begins in a corridor

This could be a room, but it's not a room, it's a hallway with Lincrusta wainscoting, a Pullman-style corridor, dark brown embossed with vertical lines and fleurs-de-lys in broad, measured rows. It's a highchair in a brown place, a length of space between seasons, between epochs, momentums. Two parallel walls where only a mother and a small child, the reason, a space where coal, a coal stove, is a keen continuous olfactory factor. It is a photograph. Everything here is black and white, though brown is here too. A need that is placed, certainly needed, a mindset where no one else, a length of time before anyone else at all, anyone else is not needed in this first, this infinite time, semi-conscious, though certainly much is nascent in first biological cells, even an echo, a pleasant echo, but not needed here. So little is needed in this place, a pleasant and sacrosanct place where only smooth, between food and warmth inside blankets, and very little is asked, where sleep and whole milk and sweet pudding and a small silver spoon, small with a perfectly curved silver handle, bent round for a baby to grip. No need for another, even though later, another might be. Where only two, a mother and a small child, very small, that might fit into the L of an elbow, very pleasant and kind.

In the beginning was noise and a flash

in anger my sister begins her small life in tumult and noise saying now
saying hers saying her first feeling recollects fury
her first act is tears
loud memory she says
she says she recalls she is crying and my mother
is trying to comb her wet baby-fine hair
for the photograph the official newspaper portrait
the photographer arriving
Harry Kitts is his name
his camera his tripod
he is setting up in the living room
I wear a white dress with short puffy sleeves
smocked with small violets printed over the fabric
no one will know they are mauve with tiny green leaves
no one will know
she's been crying all morning

later decades later when I look at the picture
we are perched black and white on the windowsill in the living room
a narrow space
my left leg hangs over the sill where Henry Kitts has arranged it
in the photograph the small scattered flowers
her hair is still wet in the picture she is smiling
almost smiling
the violets   the small leaves on my dress
each one is grey

It begins in a driveway

The first time I laid eyes on her I knew. Brash sure, haughty maybe,
a little bit crazy to claim something like that, like I could forecast the
future. I was not yet six. Maybe I exaggerate. It was decades ago. When
memory works it works to highlight, reify patches of past. The fact is I
knew. Yet if she was pivotal how does it happen that later I will let her
vanish into the void.

Which I did not know when I saw her for the first time that day end
of May '52, end of her driveway. She remained in my life until I moved
across town, our connection loosening over time, but the impress of her
never gone.

When she becomes lost no one will know where she is. Her two sisters
will be lost too. All three of them disappearing into the thin air of grown
up. Her parents gone. Her aunt. Her hair her blue eyes her backbone
steely as petrified wood.

•

Pat Hurdle became my best friend, my first, unless you count Donna Lipton, which I don't, even though Donna Lipton lived in the flat one floor below in the three-storey walk-up in Verdun where I spent the first five years of my life—and if I played with anyone before I was five, I played with her, as opposed to my new baby sister, another Donna, who cried and wouldn't do what my mother wanted her to.

I don't count Donna Lipton because of the time she mocked Mary, my favourite doll, full-sized. So full-sized, Mary was almost a real child. That day, Donna Lipton had a friend visiting from five streets away, a kid I didn't know. Their mothers were drinking tea in Donna Lipton's kitchen. Donna and her friend were drinking tea in the patchy backyard. Their tea wasn't real.

My mother was upstairs in our flat wrestling my baby sister. Mary and I were not invited to the tea party in the backyard and when I thumped down the back stairs hoping to play, the two tea-drinking friends mocked Mary, large yes, but not, as they scorned, fat. This signalled the end of my non-friendship with Donna Lipton. They even had a tablecloth on the little table set up on the dirt.

When Donna Lipton called Mary fat, I raced back up the metal stairs, Mary by the hand, her head bumping each step. She didn't mind. I banged on the back door, screaming for my mother. Who didn't come. I banged and banged. I stopped: a change of strategy was needed. I began to imagine my way around the block to our front door. I imagined walking with Mary to the end of the lane, we could make it all on our own, and then turn left and then left again into the street, a half block to the front of my building. I'd recognize my building with its attached sides, and our apartment on the second floor. I had to keep moving. I got halfway down the stairs, when my mother flung the door open.

Where two years before were trilliums and sycamore trees

my parents move us to a new place
far out of town
mud and the scent of drying cement
the edges of the front steps still razor-sharp

it makes them feel safe   my parents
a cut above   as if
they've arrived   the new street is a circle   as if
they will never no longer not
belong   in the future
I will do what I can

At five I moved into a small brand-new bungalow in Dorval, in a new
subdivision on the West Island, leaving Donna Lipton behind. She was a
year younger anyway. This suburb was middle class. My mother began
to use aluminum pots. She started to dye her hair platinum blonde. She
went to Lil's hair salon/kitchen Friday mornings to have her hair set.

We moved into our new house in October, '51. The everywhere-mud
oozed like black oil, so deep you could lose a boot, a leg if you were
under five. My sister at three had to be carried in and out of the house
until sod was laid in the spring.

Our house was located in the curved elbow where Green Circle turned
into Handfield Circle, on a large corner lot that would soon be bound by
a reluctant cedar hedge. Our picture window gave us a wide-angled view.
To the right of the front door, a blue spruce tried its best, along with a
fledgling apple tree, a baby mock orange, and a small maple in the side
yard.

In the spring, the sod, laid like tiles, tried to take hold. Pat moved into
the house one door down on the right, on the Green Circle side of our
house, next door to the Shums, who were fusty cantankerous Brits, and
who had no children except John Jr., in his twenties, who owned a racing-
green MG, and who did not speak to children. His mother and father
didn't speak to us either. My father didn't speak to them, especially not
to old Mr. Shum, John Sr. A cedar hedge planted itself between the High
Anglican Shums and my Irish Catholic father. The hedge kept everyone
safe. Our neighbours on the Handfield Circle side were German. My
father didn't speak to them either, especially not to Mr. Grope. My father
made an exception for Mrs. Grope, who would later tan in her yellow

bikini at poolside in her backyard. The Gropes had the first backyard pool. My sister and I could watch her browning from our bedroom window. In the '50s no one understood the dangers of tanning.

●

Pat moved in at the end of the week, eight months after I moved to
the street. A new family. We were five little girls at loose ends after
hopscotch, running down the street. The family milling getting used
to their driveway. The father eyeing the house. I eyed Pat and she eyed
me back unafraid. A good sign. Her sister twisted away to avoid our ten
little girl eyes. Her name was Susan, their mother said. She sucked on
the pointy end of her pigtail and laced her free hand into the hem of her
mother's tweed skirt. I loved her shyness. Pat stood firm, my height, and
though blonder than blonde I could tell she was mine.

●

Neither Green Circle nor Handfield were true circles. Together they formed an ellipsis, like the elliptical paths of the planets that orbit the sun. The Law of Ellipses.

●

The Gropes' pool was the envy of the neighbourhood, but it wouldn't exist for at least another five years. By then, some of the Circlers circled down to Florida in winter, catching their planes at the airport nearby. Mrs. Grope too. The perfect tan. She died of skin cancer.

Pat became mine and I hers   a shared party line   house to house   by fluke   nothing like that could be planned   we didn't need to dial each other's phone numbers to say hello   we used some simple party line code that I can't quite remember and like magic I'd be talking to her one house away.

My family phone was bolted to the kitchen wall midway up near the backdoor   top of the basement stairs   I could tug the coiled telephone cord round the door frame and sit on the top stair so no one could hear.

Sometimes I'd pick up the phone to make a call and there'd be a Hurdle on the line to someone else   I'd replace the receiver with care so not to listen in   so not to be heard.

When Pat and I were on the phone sometimes we'd read each other magazine articles just to stay on the line   lengthening the connection.

A Brief History of Childhood

we are ever fools
and thirsty
—Len Anderson

A child gathers answers

Sixty-Three Green Circle Melrose one-one-seven-five-two my locational
numbers plus one baby sister for free a mother for safety and a blue car
for long drives and one father at work leaving in the blue car morning
a Dodge as well as dodge ball and hopscotch skipping ropes skipping
Hopalong Cassidy how about a date meet you at the corner at half-past eight in
the street *stando* yelling *stando* against a brick wall roller skates hide-and-
go-seek answers in school also the pressure cooker beef stew steamed
lemon pudding the creek behind McTavishes' house up-on-the-hill train
tracks which a child cannot walk near the golf course where toboggans
in winter and brown strap-on rubber boots in the spring saddle shoes tap
shoes toe shoes white bucks Pat Boone gumshoe Nancy Drew rubber
soles and cartwheels and handstands though at night devils clawed the
closet and snakes rustled under the bed despite *now I lay me down to* red
rover red rover Red River coats and red Red River mittens grade one
grade two grade three a party line a best friend.

A woman gathers questions

How does the leaf know how does Turkish Finnish Kurdish French
where do numbers whence negative why and whence zero is it fact or
concept how instinct neurons for instance quarks cockroaches rats for
instance mirrors mirror cells the Mariana Trench how many creatures
will never be seen soufflés pavlova pavlovae how cells know how on
earth friends the cosmos how far back where did she go what means
without any start missing and end without end without start quantum
physics theoretical higher math mathematics how the Big Bang string
theory the CERN Synchrocyclotron Stephen Hawking how does a friend
falling off with Einstein altogether the Earth why and which equations
and how mainly from where.

First family: semi-functional answers

1.
we weren't a happy family *Father Knows Best* nothing like that
but we weren't unhappy either
anxious maybe   there was a little neglect   they didn't read to us
or tell us stories at bedtime
we never learned to mop floors or bake cakes
or send thank-you notes to aunts and to uncles
for the silver teaspoons and the comic books
I sucked my thumb until I turned twenty-three

2.
there is simple solace in the written word
which is not the solace of lambs in meadows
gambolling unafraid for their preconscious lives
it is not the solace of sea turtles   feet awkward anchors
swimming against all expectation
nor is it the solace of trees
light as green foam   nor creek song   nor a red-shafted flicker
its butt a white exclamation   nor is it the certainty of brick
nor a milkweed's soft spill from its winter-hard case
no   the written word signifies simply
we aren't alone

3.

what life gives us are things that will disappear
photographs   stories an old aunt reels out again and again
as though fishing for love
even the stories   even the aunt

there is a walk-up in Verdun near the old Lachine canal
second floor on the left where my father witnesses
me and my invisible friends   I am talking   telling them
he never forgets the menace of that   I am three
he recalls both their names   I do not

the open metal stairs   the clang of boots ringing on each metal step
and through the risers the sight of the snow churned to mud

4.

each morning waking into this house on the coast
it could be the last
after the dark there is simply the half-light of day

everything passes   a moth unable to land
unsettled in unsettled air   voices
on the morning sidewalk   disembodied   almost singing
saying *last night* saying *maybe today*
trailing away   early
and the crows have started to fight

5.
for awhile he brings home cinnamon buns
my father after work Friday nights
hot in a brown butter-stained bag   that's all

for all the years I lived with him he paid
scant attention
is that the reason I can't conjure myself
invisible as my long-lost first friend

6.
there were metal stairs and a front room
and invisible friends with odd-sounding names and cinnamon buns
there was a mother with black-circled eyes
a baby who cried and a fever and a doctor at night
a car door that slammed on my hand
a red-headed boy   maybe fifteen
they smashed his red head
into the brick wall at the end of the lane
said my father one night to my mother

7.
I was there in the kitchen
I can see that wall still   dead-end   everything brick
red
there were always those kinds of fights

●

You were in the parlour talking to them
when he happened by—he never forgot
the fright of that
he remembered their names—Rolly and Jay
but you have forgotten
you are forced to invent them
he's no longer alive

No question should go unanswered

Now if I think of the earth's origins, I get vertigo. When I / think of its death, I fall. —C. D. Wright

genesis   the first problem of first   hydrogen and carbon
firestorms   of wanting the answer
even Einstein and time   sand   handfuls of clay
layers of turtles on turtles on patriarchs   white-bearded
or blue-skinned   the problem of
black-holed or string-theoried   strung out   as in
this happens only inside your mind
the problem of inside your mind
of numbers   poeticized   epic or lyric
ravenous   abstract   as in zero   as in
not enough concrete images in the lines of this poem
the problem of not enough   infinity versus finitude
fleece clouds   full moon full gauzy white in broad day
the problem of unsolvable becoming almost convincing   flimsy
origins without origin
in the beginning already the word
mysterium   mysteriosa   unnerving   nervosa
that no one knows
infuriosa   even using very high mathematics
the problem of
very high mathematics

●

When Nancy Drew, the famous girl sleuth, received the first invitation from the United Nations to solve The Mystery of the Universe, she declined, citing inadequate math skills and no knowledge of physics, classical or theoretical. She had never studied cosmology and her marks in algebra were not outstanding, despite evening consultations with Ned, her boyfriend at the time. Not that algebra would have helped, or even geometry, in which she excelled. Also, she pointed out, she was more accustomed to solving mysteries that started with at least one dead body. She had already solved *The Bungalow Mystery* which delighted the Green Circle girls who all lived in bungalows with their own mysteries. She had also solved *The Mystery at Lilac Inn* and *The Secret of Shadow Ranch*. And so, though her track record was substantial, in all good conscience, she could not accept the UN's invitation regarding the origins of the Universe. Not yet. She thanked Mr. Bryce, the caller from the UN, and placed the phone back in its cradle.

Thus, The Mystery of the Universe remained unsolved, although several scientists, Albert Einstein included, were curious and tried. The old tropes of theological geneses were wearing thin. So, eventually, Carolyn Keene, whoever she or they might be, or have been, would set her courageous girl detective, Nancy, to work on this mystery too.

I can't say how I knew she'd be my best friend, how she would shape me as much as my mother shaped me or my father. Not that I knew what a best friend could do or undo. I only knew she could be a fairy, a fairy queen, or the kind of angel we perched on top of the Christmas tree every year, spun glass for hair.

It was late spring when they arrived, the newly planted trees not yet in leaf. If there was sun that day, it was filtered. There was a slight breeze.

I walked onto their driveway, a scrum of small neighbourhood girls behind me, crossing the line that divided the asphalt from the driveway's tarred surface. Her family piled out of their station wagon. The oldest— my size, my age, my kind of kid even though her hair was princessy blonde. I didn't know how to connect with that kind of blonde, I still don't, but it matters less now.

These distinctions of identity. This new girl had blue very blue eyes. I had the same problem with blue eyes as I had with ultra-blonde hair. My aunts sang me the chorus of a popular song, *Beautiful beautiful brown eyes, I'll never love blue eyes again* in case I felt sorry for my own plain medium-browns. Maybe that's what made me want her. Whatever it was, by the time I left their driveway that day, after a peek at the baby wrapped up in a white blanket in her mother's arms, after a sideways glance at Pat's other sister, I knew.

Twelve basic interrogative fragments

1. In the beginning?
2. Was there?
3. What about now?
4. Egg first or chicken? Salad, with or without mayonnaise?
5. Was mayo invented or was it discovered?
6. Whole wheat or gluten free?
7. Which word was *the* word?
8. What about forever?
9. What means: no beginning?
10. What constitutes friend? First, best, last, worst?
11. Acquaintance?
12. What about unanswered, unanswerable?

Girls: The Green Time

write down what you can
in whatever notation you have,
and pass it on
                                      —Len Anderson

●

Pat Hurdle
Arleen McCart
Susan Hurdle
Donna McCart
Miriam Bartleman
Judy McTavish
Judy Palmer
Barbara Palmer
Susan McTavish
Peggy Townsend
Patsy Smith
Pammy Thomson
Lynn McTavish
Lizzy Hurdle
Marnie Mustard
Leslie Oldacre
Mary Jane Tatlock
Mary Jane Norris
Antje Grope
Sylvie Gagné

Games

suppose a rope suppose linear   a trope is not always   not
necessarily round   not a birthday   a cake hiding ten shining dimes
not a celebration   a rope might be plastic   it could be red
or it could be made of brown hemp   long enough and an occasion to
jump
an occasional recourse to hold something or someone   or lasso
there is always an end to hold   sometimes two   if there are two ends
two girls must hold   one at each end of the span

if there is chalk there might be a game   hopping   into squares or
accidentally
not into squares   the squares are numbered
then they are hopped   over or into   sequentially   hope always hovers   a
friend
is always hopeful   at the top   under a curved line
the word *HOME*
and a smooth stone   if there is a phone
there is assonance   and a party line
a party line is not always a party   or political   the phone
is Bakelite   necessarily at that time black   chalk is white
or it might be yellow cylindrical   chalk is to sock
as thistle is to ditch   or whistle   stitch is to knot as clot is to cream
which is not the case here
suppose the sock is navy blue   paired   it could be a white sock
with a short cuff   the sort of sock that can be worn into a classroom

the game might be considered friendly   if apple   if thistle
if thistle in spring   it might include fairies   if unfriendly
there will be repercussions   a customary sadness   spoons too

can be friendly   an indication of alphabet soup
and marbles   glass   zero round blues
cat's eyes and zero round translucent greens

more than five friends takes a great deal of time
more than five marbles makes a respectable game
no one played jacks

Firsthand

In the inside there is deluge, on the outside there is missing. Somewhere
is refuge. Quickening. Listen. Let is-ness then be the business, let
mothers into story if only for a few more years. If quickening, there may
be answers, wind, chance literation, chance marriages, misfits, chance the
first chance, do not reprove the child asking questions. Let blue angora
mittens, a black cat, second fiddle. There is a second layer, liar, liar,
pants on fire. Never mind, there is always porridge with a sift of salt and
garbage bins under the sink whispering misery in an off-key pitch. Cinch
your belts, no one here is as rich as you may wish. Hey diddle, diddle, kit
and kaboodle, cows, spoons, a cat in a fix. In the inside there are two. In
the outside, there is one and one sitting, unseeing what will be missing.
Heaven whistles by in its finite fevered way, tin whistle stops and lingerie,
saxifrage and lingering, and tips. Q-tips. Second storey is higher than
first, pinch me if I'm wrong, never mind, the second story is typically too
blue, too long.

Circle as ellipsis

Green was the Circle's true name
half-ellipsis was the circle's true shape
orbiting the bungalowed brick   spawning girls
all the girls wore jackets of green   fairy lore
woven leaves mosses and pale fescue grasses
a green mesh of girls   friendships and fights
some wished for flight   every birthday
when they blew out their candles they wanted to fly
I make half of this up   some wished for kindness
a new dress   a good mark   their average number was twice
their combined average age   half-flying
half-fairies   half-launching from the small mound of a hill
beyond the street's elliptical orbit
behind the ring of northside houses   their hair spuming
spinning milkweed in spring sometimes burred
a world within worlds   in their mouths
were thin greenstick twigs
pussy willows   sumac   marbles   pink bubble gum
their teeth were small and imperfect
their shoulder blades   wing bones   unfeathered
their feet rubber-soled

13. Do fairies have wings?
14. Magical, spacious as sky?
15. Imaginary?
16. Governed by Queens?
17. Before humans or elves?
18. Silver coins for bloodied first teeth?
19. Changelings for children?
20. Green jackets or red? Fiction or fashion?
21. Gay speculation?
22. If you don't see them, are they still in the green woods?

In the dream I drive along Church Avenue, past Martin Avenue, and over the small bridge onto Green Circle. Circling back. A friend in the passenger seat, short hair, wearing a silk scarf. *This is where I grew up*, I tell her. *These bungalows are so old*, she says. But the brick walls look fresh to me in their angled tangled green gardens, and some houses have been recently reno'd.

I wonder if I'll be able to locate Pat Hurdle's old house, and yes, I know it by its place in the row of houses as I drive slowly by, one down from my old red brick house, and also by the white birch, taller now than the roof, and by the old Ponderosa in the front yard. The house doesn't look like its old self. Completely refurbished, I decide. Past the Shums'. Then we stop in front of my old bungalow, which doesn't resemble its former self either. Immediately an aged couple in the back seat, who have been there all along, unobserved and silent, get out, want to walk. It's been a long ride. The street, the houses, something about the air, looms ominous.

Peggy and Mrs. Townsend walk out of their house, approach us, bigger than life. Everything on this street is now larger than life. And colourful. The bricks so orangey-red close-up, they look almost on fire.

They say yes, no, do not let the old couple go. Already we know the old couple will be taken away if they wander about on their own. A sense of surveillance closes in. I ask Peggy if she will vouch for the old couple if they are picked up. And yes, she will. She says the street has been bought by a German gold-mining company which maintains tight security. We are incredulous. A German gold-mining company? But this is the global economy; anything can be bought, anything can happen. My sister is with me, and my wife. Pat Hurdle is not. She's been missing for years.

●

Can a sister be causal   can a friend
can a room or a closet
a quark or a photon cause
a heart's course
through the night

nor was she compliant   my sister   limits were set
she paid no attention to the space where serpents were finally found
she was even confined to the house
which she enjoyed for a time   top spot

was it a cat I saw or a devil with four furry paws
she always wanted a dog   she always bit into a wrist
if a wrist was presented
with every one of her small razor-sharp teeth

Mrs. Hurdle takes twelve hopeful dolls to the orphanage

O, orphines,
you unmothered unfathered girl children
who occupy thin side-by-side beds on the third floor
of the mission-style monolith at the end of the long narrow road
off Côte-de-Liesse

we can't see you wave   we can't see you smile

did you unwrap your gift dolls onto your pillows
remove their handmade skirts from the shoeboxes
we measured to fit
wrapped in tissue and red cellophane
a skiff of soap in the corner to scent their used vinyl skin

we small mothered fathered bungalowed girls
with toy sewing machines want to know if you

pity rising like rain   and fear
rinsing our small buttered hearts

she took the twelve dolls
placed and prepared
she said
to the orphanage mid-December

did they arrive? did you unwrap them?
did you see them at all?

Green Circle had no corners   nowhere   no commas   no periods
nowhere to hide   just the continual elliptical round   even if I say *at the*
corner of Handfield and Green I mean only to say adjacent   meaning where
the names merge   street or family names where memory exists   my
middle name inside the name of my aunt inside the name of her aunt
names exist   blue suede shoes exist on Ed Sullivan's show merging with
Elvis   Mrs. Booth's curly fries emerge in her kitchen   Suzanne Pleshette
in my mind   no one wrote anything in our family   as if we were
illiterate   therefore memory prevails as Plato said   except shopping lists
maybe and Christmas cards   except my homework   after which my hair
in a flip required the application of rollers   colossal   with brushes and
plastic picks to hold the rollers in place against the skin at the sides of my
face   all night the picks rivet the edge of my forehead and cheeks while
the metal brush rollers transmit a low-frequency pitch from outer space
where answers exist   merge   the flip held through the day   a hopeful
springing up round my head.

•

If I say my second name   a name without public presence   a name
meant only to link   I mean only to say it merges into an odd nominal
lineage   Lyda   great aunt   aunt   me   my mother not liking her
aunt but liking her sister her oldest who died crossing a snow-packed
Laurentian road wearing skis when a car   a teacher and oldest though
not the first   the first died when she was two   Aunt Lyda   martyr   she
could have saved the whole family   my mother included.

•

In the new-day-experimental-research dream
the woman gives birth to two birds
an ordinary woman with no sign of wings
the birds are small   dark and unfeathered
they signify nothing
when I open my window
despite days of crazy-sick heat
there is snow on the branches
blackbirds and patches of white on the ground

●

First-born is caution is hubris is love first love
cancels the dark of the morning
first fear begins
slithers first devils first snakes first animated Disney escape
Pinocchio leaves through the high narrow window
turns into an ass   a donkey   first breath   still breathing
again first fear shadows first memory
first story tracks what's remembered
alters recall   first question reveals
longing
the curious significance of first
green jackets   call and response   first friend   two hands in a clasp
two halves of a clamshell   peas in a pod
first answer folds
first friend is an answer   a way to belong

Rules for street fighting

no biting
said my mother
no fists   no slapping   not cheeks face or head
no pinching
no pushing   into creeks into streets
down the stairs   no kicking
heads   stomachs   ankles or knees

but pulling hair   yes
said Mrs. Hurdle
ponytail   pigtail   any length   any fistful
of hair   a yank   a firm tug
leaves no visible mark

First place

There is contest without fail, comparison, three judges, a kind of race.
Human. There is winning. There is mutton and milk, mushy peas and
mulligatawny soup. There are seconds. Would you like more mashed
potato? There's second place which is better than third but not the real
prize pitch perfect the big hurrah ho ho the hearty har har the business
end the point the first place. Second is not a real place not lasting
pleasure, it's not a golden-thirds classical composition happy face, heart,
cabbage on the plate with sufficient sweet yellow butter. Red roasted
beef and almost blue and underdone and maybe there's blood. An oil
painting, it is not. The sky looks down. Pass me a full slice of life.

After they moved in, I went to their house, invited inside one Saturday morning through the front door. A new world. The rugs in the front hall were thick, the living-room walls festooned with boughs of red maple leaves. CBC morning radio murmured from two large speakers hanging in the far corners of the dining room. There were area rugs in the living room too, Persian, not that I knew Persian rugs at the time, or even CBC radio, but I understood the solemnity of the place, the modulated voices from the radio speakers, the rich winey colours laid on the floor.

These days we might call this *cultural capital*. I admired the Tom Thomson print over the sofa, not that I knew Tom Thomson, and the spray of fall leaves mounted over the print. I wanted to live in this house. I wanted this mother, and this shy sister too. I would even have tolerated the baby and the father who was too lanky and who didn't speak, not that fathers had ever to speak. Mostly, I wanted this mother, maybe not to replace my own—I loved my own—but I wanted a share. Surely, this was not so much to ask.

In the spring and fall, Pat's mother led us into the woods across the CPR tracks, five or eight little girls trailing behind her as she pointed out trillium and milkweed and pussy willow. She showed us mushrooms on the underside of wet bark and bird nests in the arms of old trees, skunk cabbage, puff balls, dead moles, minnows in the creek bed, silver birch, white birch, sumac bunching into blood-coloured bloom. All the jewelled, wooded wonders.

The other mothers on the street played bridge. My mother belonged to three bridge clubs. In the afternoons the other mothers sewed collars on dresses with their new sewing machines. They knit mittens and Mary

THE PAPER HOUND BOOKSHOP
344 PENDER ST W
VANCOUVER   BC

ARD   ***********5011
ARD TYPE   INTERAC
CCOUNT TYPE
              FLASH DEFAULT
ATE   2022/02/15
IME   5745 17:56:03
ECEIPT NUMBER
H84075923-001-523-007-0

URCHASE
OTAL

          $12.60
----

nterac
0000002771010
8E76CF64B195DA1
080008000-

APPROVED
UTH# 645640   00-001
HANK YOU

     CARDHOLDER COPY

Maxim sweaters for us to wear when winter arrived. They knew winter would always arrive. Most of the time they were relieved to have the children out of the house during the day, out of sight. They knew the end of the day would come soon enough.

●

Not belonging to Pat's family but thinking I could. Might be welcome. But that evening when Mrs. Hurdle gave her three daughters dishes of canned peaches to eat in the bedroom where we were playing Crazy Eights on the floor, there was no dish for me. Not enough peaches in the tin, explained Mrs. Hurdle. I was there only for a short card game before I went home to bed. I was an outsider, as if a foster child. If I could belong at all, it would be as a foster.

Second hand

If there's a split, there must be a firsthand way to fit in, to sit, to ditch whatever's unfit, to quit, to quieten the ifs, initiate whens. If there is a firsthand way, it is a roar, a trip, trip-trop, a visit, a kind of tryst, a tête-à-tête. First is the intimate, the true top. And if there's a first hand, there must be a zero hand, a hand with nothing in it, a hand-me-down-the-emptiness, a flick, flit, a now-you-see-it trick and now-you-don't, tick tick, tick tock, the mouse, the digital. With zero hour, second hand, no clock.

Black holes

Once upon a time a child dreamt of a child who was herself. Not just once or twice, or even three times. In the dream, recurring, the child hears a knock at her front door. Middle of the night. She gets up to answer. Again, no one else in the house is awake. Why can't her parents hear the knock at the door? Because this is a dream. She crosses the living-room floor, the green wall-to-wall, in her bare feet. The world is full of quiet suburban night. Nothing outside the big picture window but emptiness and street lamps. Yes, she is nervous, but she pulls open the door, peaks around the edge of the door. And there, hunched, with a basket in her hand, is an old woman. Some might call the old woman a witch, though she wears no pointy hat. The child knows it's a witch. Later in life she will learn about witch burnings and will change her mind about witches altogether. But she is still young in this dream and this witch is not necessarily friendly. The night lies behind the old woman, vast and somehow otherworldly, and the old woman's face is not the face of someone the girl knows, though she will see her again and again in this very same dream. The child pushes but finds she can't close the front door. Then, and this is the worst part, she begins to fall through the floor. The wood splinters under her feet, and she falls into the basement. Part way. Scrambles up. Over and over, falling and rising, again and again. She cannot stand firm.

Later, she learns this is a dream that children without sufficient rules might suffer. Lawless.

My mother set only one rule: no singing at the table. We never sang at the table. My father set no rules at all, although he was frequently critical.

Daisy chain I

he loves me my father he loves me not
he knows not how to or what he can love

he sees me my father he sees me not
his eyes rest instead on the wings

of newsprint in his two ham-ish hands
he drives a blue Dodge flanked with chrome

the blue is robin's-egg blue I love his blue car
I watch how he darts through lanes of big-city traffic

how his body rocks weaving in weaving out
I love him I love him not

I will not know what in him there is to love
until each petal is pulled

Daisy chain II

she loves me she loves me she loves
me   in the photograph I wear a live daisy

daisy chain I made in the morning
round my neck   holding it up

away from the bodice of my pale yellow dress
as if to say white and yellow-green

though the photograph is only grey   black and white
I hold the chain up   delicate   I hold it with care

out from the dress she made for me
my mother

yellow satin an overskirt of soft-yellow net
pale as winter sun

as primula   chiffon   lemon curd
which is how I know about love

she made the dress   she is the chain

•

Pat's granddaughter aged four tells Pat
when we were dead my sister and me
our father was still a little boy
you were with him then under the covers
hiding
there was a bat flying in the room
and you were hiding   yes

once all of them were dead
Pat and her son once and her two granddaughters
a bat in the room   they were all hiding

•

At the end of June, Mrs. Hurdle would drive us to the municipal pool in Lachine, an outdoor swimming pool, grey unpainted aggregate, no deep end for diving, no smooth poolside surface for tanning on towels. Just bunches of wild kids racing around in faded swimsuits, splashing, yelling, mostly in French, mostly boys. A whole other world. Lachine. But Mrs. Hurdle, just that she was with us as we walked onto the loud cement surface, made it okay.

It turned out that public pools contributed to the spread of polio. Rampant in the early fifties. Scores of children affected. Salk wouldn't save us until 1955. By then two kids on our street were already living with the sequelae of polio. My mother told me. Judy, my age, and Peter, a year younger, both softer somehow than the rest of us. Polio floated their steps, gentled their grip, slowed their pace. They lived in the slightly off-centre kingdom of illness. It was hard to know how to slow down enough to be with them. These phyla of difference, hierarchical youth.

●

Pat's mother went jewelless   my mother
wore rhinestones to divide night from the day

Pat's mother knew where pussy willows turned into cats near the CPR
   tracks
my mother kept the deep fryer on the back of the stove

her hair was champagne   her fancy heels were four inches high
Pat's mother wore brogues

and drove a station wagon long as a long flat-bed truck
piled with neighbourhood kids   no seat belts   no one got hurt

I wanted them both   Pat's mother   my own   each in the right place
my mother loved me without saying   sewed me dresses

and yellow net tutus for the show in the spring
each mother stayed in her place

for as long as she could
for as long as their bodies allowed

In which the new girl is punished for being new

there is preference   there is friction   fear   there is mathematics
which is not heart to heart but is nonetheless a strain of language
there is two plus two but not in this Universe
infliction yes   initiation   intimidation
and a skipping rope
no one knows the particular inducement that day
three girls with a plastic rope does not equal one girl with none
does not equal skipping though a skipping rope that day was used
silent almost silent at the start
at the end
on the legs and arms around the waist not so much her face
there was silence in the street
the rope was red   it carved a high S in the air
in the chase
a banquet of girlish pique
boredom fear hunger it was five o'clock
finally
from an opened door a mother's call
to dinner
they hardly used their hands   none ever said
springtime in dying sun
none could see even her shadow

●

Pat letting a cat into my mother's kitchen sneaking it in just to see my
mother's alarm how she'd run for the bathroom   lock the door.

Mischievous or unkind or maybe just curious   maybe curiosity   vaunted
by Einstein   exonerates a child.

Whatever it was made her do it I know that humanity the whole
ferocious range of it entered our young bones early   on that off-circular
street.

Equal time

in the dream it's nighttime as it is nighttime
in real time in the real house
in the real house my mother sleeps in a room down the hall
in the dream she could be in paradise
washing dishes
tea towel damp on her left shoulder
she could be on the phone cigarette in her hand
smoke like wings over her head   her nails painted fire-house red

she is not in the dream when I float into my sister's room
I am nineteen or twenty or
beyond numbered age
my sister has just finished high school
I take her in my arms she
is no longer crying
my sister in the dream
my mother in paradise
I take my sister into my arms

Soul of the world

in the drawing   crayon on Protestant School Board newsprint
large standard issue
the woman is pushing the baby carriage into the future   the baby
does not look concerned
facing the mother facing the past
this could go almost anywhere
the seven-year-old artist pushes the story past the paper's right edge
presses hard with the green
rocking on time's uncertain fulcrum
having reached the purported age
of reason   about to want
explanations   halfway between inside and out
despite appearances her past contains certain dark ages   edges
and though some say that time no longer exists
we still ask   where are they going   that blithe baby
mother and carriage
where are they on their way to
aiming right off the page

Nothing is happening

as night decreates day   ink wash on ink wash on ink wash
falls   this dark   this division   winter nights begin in late afternoon
I am eight years old   snowbank   snow fort
late late afternoon and I raise an icicle   frozen telescope to my freezing
    right eye
pierce through to the stars   back to the start
the first
the Planck epoch is not start enough   so many constellations

so young I am freed time to time from the cupola of clocks
now swathed in mountains of snow
as snow buries the place from where I comb the navy-blue sky
what stands in for a roof

all things can be imagined   all things can be known   this is not true
for sure   that division   first from the rest   for sure
the glass square in the bricks of the house lights up behind me
amber and steam   I don't have to look   far
as the far chinks in the vast dark over my head   that house
my dinner is being prepared   but not yet   stay
stay inside the billowed blanketing white

ice cube is to star as here is to unknowing
for sure I'm alone   stuck inside time   if not
then what   how to locate infinity
a cubist face is to a child's face as time is
to the face of the world
what rhymes with the word
pearl-hued or cold   absurd   white gauze or fast   soft

the sound of rice in a sieve
breath of a fish under ice

•

One day on my way home from Dorval Gardens School the year before
I was made to change to St. Joseph's I was eight crunching snow beneath
my brown rubber boots.

The AM radio in the kitchen that morning broadcast news that a child's
body had been found stuffed into a trunk chopped up.

I said to myself out loud so I could hear my own promise not to kill
children when I grew up worried I might forget what it was like to be a
child receiving that kind of news what it was like to once be a child.

Cosmologies

those winter nights   the stars replete
as though seen from the Sahara   we lived in a suburb
a form of desert   fathomless space   miles of linoleum   sandless
tarred driveways   crazy eights   ordinary matter
which is what we are made of   gravity   light   the stars
those nights
sweet points on black   a freight train blowing straight through
behind the north line of houses
every night   hauling   howling through the suburban flatlands
the silent nowhere of this almost empty terrain
the speed of the train flatlined under the stars   railcars   thunder dogs
a comfort
as the stars were a comfort   their shine so real around us
wonder and roof

Cosmos

This flaw in everything—not
even nothing is perfect
                    —Len Anderson

The day of the Big Bang, or a sudden change of schools

I wonder if this is how the neutrinos felt before the cosmic Big Bang, as they hung out that day on the dark side of nothing, knowing nothing of what was imminent, before everything was thrown into mass chaotic action. Going about their business, eating their ordinary neutrino toast and jam breakfast that day, say, when their father scrapes his chair back from the table and says, *Hurry up, neutrinos, I'm driving you to school this morning.* He's never done that before. Some kind of big shakeup: we're throwing the switch in five minutes. September 5th, first day of grade four, 1955, and the little sister neutrino says, *Do I have to eat all my crusts?*

Albert Einstein died five months before. The little sister has not been paying attention. But the older sister neutrino knows something's up and says, *What?* to the mother, who lowers her sad neutrino eyes. The father says, *I'm driving you to the Catholic School this morning. St. Joseph's.* And that's the story of the Big Bang as they know it. But there's more.

We'd gone to Protestant schools all our elementary lives. Dorval Gardens School is brand spanking new. Our friends are there. Our desks are there. Our teachers are there, waiting. We only know about St. Joseph's School because Judy McTavish, who lives across the street, goes to St. Joseph's with her younger brother, Danny. They are Catholic. We are not. Until now. That division: Catholic neutrinos, Protestant neutrinos. We are about to enter a fierce cosmic expansion. Colossal. Firestorms and black holes. We are the confusion.

Pat Hurdle waited for me on her doorstep for twenty minutes that September 5th morning, feeling somehow ashamed, she told me later, much later, that I'd forgotten to meet her. That I didn't show up. My father was driving us. The wrong way to the wrong school. I forgot everything that morning, even my best friend, Pat, waiting. To meet as we had always met up to walk to school.

Eclipse

on August 21, 2017, 10:22 a.m.

already half-light   the moon sickles the sun   a scythe
day-moon upon us on the streets in diminishing light
office workers out on the street swivel their heads looking up
their hands shielding their eyes   stand with digital cameras
pinhole glasses   crouch on the sidewalk   coffee break
one worker makes a diagram on a sheet of white paper
they say every day do something new
halfway into the path of totality everyone knows
not to look at the sun but

finally she was no longer there
it took years to notice she'd gone
no one had seen her in decades
no one knew her new name
her sisters too   gone   and new names

the path of alignment   unlightenment   the gradual disappearing
summer morning and the motion-sensor light
flicks on at the head of the driveway
the sun's high in the sky but the light
dim   other-worldly shadows
scallop themselves in half crescents

half curls   small curving yods
ghosting the sidewalk cement

First Catholic school

My sister loved the holy cards, saints pictured with eyes rolled up toward heaven. She loved rosary beads and white missals with pale ribbons, placeholders in the middle of Mass. Rosary beads in varying colours: translucent red pomegranate seeds, drops of His Precious Blood, and blue, opalescent, a small silver cross at the end. Pale green or large black wooden beads, the painted wood clack-clacking from the belts of the Grey Nuns as they swished by in their heavy grey skirts. I preferred the Crucifix that hung over the altar, the mystery, the wonder of suffering we all had to bear in those days. My first Catholic friend was Jackie Brunelle. She was not Pat Hurdle. She believed none of it, not even hellfire, intrepid, nothing at all.

●

Waking up as I usually did/do in the middle of the night, anxious, as I usually was/am, concerned about assorted details, devils in the closet, snakes under the bed, and so planning a leap into my sister's safe bed an arm's-length away, as I usually did, but waking this time, mid-November, to the sound of a pen scratching on paper. Not the hot hiss of devils, the dry rustle of snakes.

She was in my room perched that night on the low padded stool that matched my dressing table, notebook in hand. I thought she could be one of the low lurking devils, but when she spoke, I noticed her New England accent, her phrasing. I'd read *The Bungalow Mystery*.

Oh, she said, *of course, you weren't expecting me. Nancy Drew, at your service*, she said.

Bungalow Mystery, I whisper back. *Mystery of the Old Clock. George and Bess. Devils in the closet?*

Nope, not anymore, she said.

You solved it?

Yes, she said, *it was easy, but I understand that you've been wondering, or will be wondering, about the origins of the cosmos. I'm here to check in. Random selection. People interested in. Even kids. Especially kids*, she said. She had her own questions.

Apart from notions, she asked, *of first day, first word, first best friend, what do you think constitutes the concept of first?* I had no idea what she was talking about. *What happens before first*, she asked. I sat up in my bed. I was nine years old. Had she asked Pat Hurdle?

I said, *Wait, you're Nancy Drew, right?* Just to make sure.

Does first not indicate a beginning, she continued, *maybe a location of sorts, a timing, something that goes before, an antecedent. And if there is* no *beginning*, she said, *what could first possibly mean?*

Never delusional as a child, and not much more now, this incident, this sighting of Nancy Drew on this page, I have to admit, might be a conceit. Which raises the question of conceit of the other variety. *Conceited* was one of the worst things you could call someone when I was growing up. Much more appealing to be considered modest, to know your place. But here is Nancy Drew, herself a conceit, evoking the issue of mystery, the unanswered, still aiming for solutions. A conceit, part of the story.

I asked, *Why?* She stopped writing. My sister did not wake up.

I've been hired to solve a mystery, she said. *It involves the cosmos.*

And I'm thinking: Oh yeah, Nancy Drew, that really *is* a little conceited.

Then Let Me Ask

The greatest strength
of any theory
or any other
kind of question
is to bring us to our knees
       —Len Anderson

The American Wilderness Act

This continent of landscapes   alpine   forest   genetic banks of trees
which one is not worth preserving   beauty yes   and renewal   prairies
too   Wallace Stegner's   his childhood loneliness   his father reaching
down always in anger   sky too reaching clear down to the ground   on
every side   weasels   badgers   burrowing owls   his Wilderness Letter
his prairie defence   the Wilderness Act and this particular claim

                                                                worth.

Then let me ask

                what is not worth preserving   what is not vanishing   as
if we are not always fading away   lonely   as if we are not all grand   our
places too   worth preserving   which one of us is not also a form of
wilderness   what about my old street risky with children   part circle
part hand   ditches and ragweed and rain   who will preserve that first
place   childhood and rows of first bungalows growing more and more
modest   and front yard trees now five times their old size.

The first question is

from where   whence   this materiality
begins
to begin   from where contrails   tails of flame flying   what before the
Big Bang
religion   theory   superstition   supersymmetry   Hadron Collider
multiverse   uni
verse   forty-six-page equations   spark   spin   sun   stars   time
how outer islands of moons   Saturn   craters   Pluto
Plato   memory   particles   waves   salt water   protozoa   protean
how out of nothing
how upright   how cortical functions
beyond what is called tangible
conscious mind or not conscious mind   from where
from what   a little bit how

How body can betray any girl

my father faulted fat people fat
people with icing on cakes   their lips moving
having their cake and eating it too
buttered bread buttered both sides buttered buns icing
the buns or cupcakes the size of the buns
Pat was not
I was almost not exactly not but listing in that direction
lemon pudding steamed in the oven hard sauce whipping
cream cake turned upside down
chocolate jelly roll cream puffs hot butterscotch sauce
so many just desserts
though I liked pork chops as well
my mother excelled as a baker

The bungalow mystery

there is always a time when little is known
which is where I have lived
my life   a time when you don't know what it is you don't know
millennia   there is a time
when you don't know what it is that you're asking
broken shells   fossils   an old fountain pen   bottled ink
a mystery   a moth   science fiction
graphic novels   Egyptian Greek Icelandic
biblical and Roman myth

Solitaire summer

almost July but still the rain rivers   the potential for rain
always present the year I turned twelve
everything wet
I was taking on religion the way a boat takes on water
a question of truth   finding an answer
the windows sluicing with wet
I cut myself off   walled myself in   a type of anchorite
no longer grouping myself   a half-child   every morning
a pack of cards on the Duncan Phyfe table splayed out in rows
a game made for rain
for beating yourself   for beating the odds   I was earnest   no cheating
no sips of rye from the bottom shelf of the Duncan Phyfe hutch
no boyfriend   no poker   no late-night Russian roulette
no slashing   no tantrums   the summer of higher calling
the meaning of life
meaning God   whatever answer lurked beyond the blurred window
I kept losing
my mother grilled the sandwiched Kraft cheese
set tea towels to soak in the sink overnight
no one asked why
every day I shuffled   reshuffled the deck

Pat was not yet fourteen when her mother died

then when the blossoms   shy on the apple
early this year   behind hedges   then when
the willow   pussies staggered along the red stems
catkins about to be reckless   undo
be undone   the maple in froth   the sumac   sycamore
the staghorn beginning to bud

then when the milkweed
how I remember the low hill
behind the McTavishes' house
the leftover pods still stiff   silver shells in the spring
everything jewelled   then
even that year

when only three months before   winter
waning   but still palpable
a presence   her mother   who had taught us
to see under the ferns   taught us the names
who many times had taken us over the tracks to the woods
while other mothers played bridge

where then
the trillium and the jack-in-the-pulpit
burrs   beggar's tick and corncockle   quaking aspen
and the thin silver birch   her mother
breast cancer   sinking   her mother
when all she had then was a window   died

●

After the birthday cake has been eaten and the small family party winds down my two-year-old granddaughter begins to stagger   well past her bedtime   street lights shine into the front window   maybe she stumbles maybe she hears it's time to go home   maybe she picks up a vibe   but something sets her to crying   though she rarely cries   her parents gather up their sweet wailing daughter and as they are leaving through the back door she asks her mother in whose arms she is riding   mum   why am I crying.

Later her mother tells me that as they walk into their house   returning home with their still-crying daughter   she asks again   mum why am I *still* crying.

I rarely cry though sometimes I feel welling under my eyes   a tenderness something that feels like connection.

Black Holes

there is only so much,
even of nothing
                        —Len Anderson

●

About Pat Hurdle's mother there was never a warning never an omen a harbinger.

In the case of my mother there were telling signs   tobacco   cigarette smoke   a wound on her leg that wouldn't heal

•

She died more than fifty-nine years ago. Cancer. Pat was almost fourteen; I was thirteen and a half. She died almost in spring, the time of year her three daughters had birthdays. 1961. Therefore, it's not possible, even in a dream, that she would now be alive. But in the dream, she's alive.

We have entered the church hall, my friend Yaana and I. Pat's informing the audience, many of whom are lesbians on their way to a party, about her mother's condition. Dire, she says, but not dead. It seems I am wrong, or partially wrong about her mother. Pat says that her face has changed, become pixilated, pointillist, more yellow points than pink, she says, but orange and blue too.

There are many things wrong. She's suffering. Yes, cancer, but I wonder if lupus is also involved. *What can be done?* I ask, and Pat says it's come down to money. For a special device or more treatments, so Yaana and I donate money. Others contribute too. We collect it in a small paper bag.

We tell Pat we'll meet her for coffee and give her the money, but the directions for the café are confusing, Yaana becomes my sister in the middle of everything, and we need to make a sharp U-turn in heavy traffic. Nevertheless, we arrive, Pat's mother still there alive. The radiance of miraculous dreams.

How numbers count

The shape of numbers is gestural, curvilinear, wild. There are lines. Circles. There are the numbers five, seven, four; there is two. There is first. Six million, eighty-three hundred. The number of numbers is without end, grows as the Universe grows, leaves on trees, rates of inflation. Numbers' uses grow every day. There is binary. Time. There is space. Space-time. Fingers and toes. They say numbers began without a beginning. There is zero, invented, discovered, cooked up. Whatever happens under cover of zero, things vanish. As though subsumed. Premature death. Or birth. There is infinity. Belief. Speculation. There is despair. What exists without being invented?

Prime numbers

Forty-six is the year we were born but forty-six is not a prime number
we can divide it many times many ways   and now knowing nothing of
each other after knowing so much for at least thirteen   years   which is
a prime number   and forty-six is twice twenty-three and twenty-three is
a prime number too   nothing can divide twenty-three but one and itself
what was it that divided us   there are two of us   also a prime number
twenty-three times two is forty-six and therefore must signify something
if numbers do pre-exist   numbers have so little of the concrete about
them   so little of the human   but angels   numberless on the heads of
numberless pins.

●

My sister saw Pat Hurdle once in a lineup outside a downtown Ottawa cinema. She can't recall the movie's name. She even talked to Pat, but my sister didn't introduce her to her husband because they were in the middle of their divorce. Maybe Pat was in the middle of a divorce too. My sister was the only one who ever saw her during those lost years. Some said she moved to Bolivia to work for Oxfam, her last name changed, married to someone nobody knew. No one knew anything. Like the Universe, she had every possible history, every possible future.

•

If a friend
            falls
                    below   beyond radar's rotating bands
scanning the world for movement in wide-arching swaths
layering the days   if
a friend   if no address
leaving   no letter   no
notice   no phone   if
                    she falls
beyond peripheries   beyond greenish-lit screens
past the edges of possibility   past fairy folk   illuminations
sea serpents   narwhals   mammoths with impossible tusks
ancient maps in old fusty books   forests like prisons
meteorites pitting Earth's surface
if this friend
years   decades   if no one knows   if only childhood
if only small photographs are left without any colour

●

Take this coat   Red River navy blue   wool with red piping and a knitted
red sash   the coat is also a river   a history   water flowing east flowing
south   take this winter   this weather   this coterie   songs and singsongs
unsung   red rover red rover we call Pat over   the age is seven or the age
might be eight   a party line then at the time   red rover red rover   we
call her back.

If calling if ever she calls us from a life in the future   the call might be
from Castro's Cuba perhaps   somewhere east somewhere south.

●

Take this bunting   lamb's wool and square and almost certainly white
shake it from mourning   moored in a pram   shake it from sleep
beware of memory   of theft   later   if heart and ego and winter and one
mother or two mothers go missing   and if lips chap in the cold   red and
rough   tears and a Red River red tasselled toque flops over the forehead
to the right or to the left   winters still bright in the mind   and ice on an
iron rail tears the first layer of tongue.

Carolyn Keene was a fiction, a syndicate name

She was more than one writer   she did not invent algebra but someone did   fairies too   someone did   changelings   but not the migrations of birds   which are also mysterious   origins too   wherever she went was a mystery for years   numbers too   their provenance   how they divide up the world   the body   think of breathing   the mind   think of neurons the way one tree talks to another   a forest   the way I talk to my mother who is dead   decomposed   the way a chrysalis   jaw-dropping   the way a baby   stars   and yet we carry on   as if nothing   as though we will know the way home.

•

The elegance of the equation is the poetry of mathematics the way
the stone arcs into the pond and ripples out   almost Fibonacci   falling
folding around itself the way songs sing themselves the way dreams
clarify at the same time confuse the Doppler effect carries sound future
and past whole numbers consist of nobility the queen of mathematics
how seesaws the balance unbalance the fall the way a first friend is
forever some numbers are called amicable paired forever are rare the way
we balance on tiny bones teeter the first time we walk we are solving the
way forward and backward the elegance of anything   into millennia.

Time is not the only proposition the only answer there are neurons in
places other than brains.

Perfect numbers multiply adding up always the same way our search for
answers our search for perfection searching for little people under blue
violets in gardens in constellations between drops of water between two
palms in darkness in darkness when crying for a glass of plain water for
someone to hold.

Later, Nancy began to work on yet another important mystery more suited to her experience and talents: to find the elusive Pat Hurdle, The Mystery of the Lost Friend. 1992. No one could say where Pat Hurdle was. Missions impossible, but Nancy was determined. She studied Pat Hurdle's bio, thankfully much shorter than that of the cosmos. She contacted each of Pat Hurdle's old friends, her teachers, elementary and high, and her skating coaches as well, even Miss Taylor, who once taught Pat tap dance and toe, and her minister, the Reverend Mr. Lorden, her Brownie leader, Carol Knight, and her Girl Guide leader, Mrs. Ann Powell.

Nice kid, some said, a little shy maybe. Smart, always first in the class. First class, said others, especially the skating coaches. Number one, said Mrs. Knight. Pat had been leader of the Fairy Troop in Girl Guides. A bit of a fairy, said one of the younger Green Circle girls, a little sneaky, said another, but that was to be expected. Haughty, according to her sister, Susan, said one of Susan's old friends. Best, said her once best friend, and her first.

●

Meanwhile, the Universe gathered around its own mystery. Nancy read on, learning to speak mathematics and book-long equations. When she wasn't interviewing Pat Hurdle's friends, she questioned top scientists, always sorry that Himself, Dr. A. Einstein, was now part of the mystery and unable to contribute in situ. She was on the scent, closing in on Pat Hurdle.

Nancy, putting two and two together, then three and three. Following the whole chain of events back to the first, first sighting in the driveway in 1952 when they spilled out of the car onto the tarmac beside their mudded lawn and the five small neighbourhood girls came running down the street. Beginning there. Nancy reconstructed everything. Missing persons was her favourite job, second only to a dead body in a haunted house. One thing leading to another. The movie theatre in Ottawa. The Palmer girls, the McTavishes, the yoga, the ashram, the government jobs, the aunt in Victoria, Miriam in Nova Scotia. Then one day . . .

●

Despite the surrounding collapse the impending increasing collapse
despite the collapse of ideas and rivers and lakes in toxic collapse despite
equations   pages and pages   virtual collapse of faith and bodies and
minds memories quietude the collapse of morality of cities their sewer
systems roads classrooms the collapse of peace talks of peace and even
logic   despite all that   from where   and what   the word   though old-
fashioned   is whence

having raised this question too many times without any answers how
did the start of the start start not so much how did trees human voices
mouths ants with antennae shining air in the summer forest ferns sword
ferns bracken and curved silver scythes books with spoiled pages water
maidenhair frost not so much meteorites giraffes sticklebacks mothers
with eyes in the backs of their heads angels perched in trees with over-
wide wings

                                        but how unconditioned origins whence
when *no worthy question is ever answered on the same plane that it was asked*
according to Einstein how to frame the question not knowing the plane
on which I must ask it and how to understand the answer even wrapped
in gold paper not being a cosmologist and no longer a child but old and
almost weary wary of the first question.

Second-hand smoke

I am now four years   almost five   past my mother
whom I have outlived   overgrown
her death
she was just sixty-eight
Rothman executives probably died too   who didn't
light up   those spirited days   rum and coke   rye and ginger
ashtrays glassy and green   big as dinner plates
big as a mother's big love   if she thought of it
she thought they'd never kill her
if she thought it at all
all that smoke in the kitchen
all that second-hand thinking

To bite into the apple

an apple might be a Spartan   red   if it's not red
it might be a Transparent
or a Cox's Orange Pippin   in each case the inside
is either white or off-white or slightly pink
the mantle and the interior are not the same
but they can be sliced in the same movement
with the same knife   sometimes in innocence
slicing   slicing can be done with intention with a sharp bone-handled
   knife
with serrations   it can be done without innocence
without any thought and with no serrations

cut   core   crescent   plate
place in a serial pattern
an overlapping circle arrangement   in this case
the apple becomes more
more interior   more layered   knowing   artful
the taste of the word
in either case the apple is blamed

•

Who mentioned abduction   who invoked aliens   who knew her married
name   who knew where to find her   Oxfam someone said   who said
Fidel   where was FB   where was the FBI the RCMP   did she miss me
as she dreamed through morning meetings or like the fairy queen was
she bucking sideways in her kitchen on her dainty twist mop   why did
it matter   was there not enough to do with the children and floors of
my own to keep clean   and yet if she disappeared   if she truly is missing
am I not missing too.

As if a cat

the missing person   the missing person poster missing too
no one could imagine her name   her first name of course
but not the last   her middle name missing even now
her cats both black and grey   her former face
her paper birch unravelling in the front yard
of her former house   her former voice
years   the range of worldwide
the eye   how far the mind
and then

and then
despite the range
of worldwide apprehension
by means of fascicle miraculous
mysterious enigmatic virtual in proportion to biblical weight
King James Version or *Ripley's Believe It or Not*   by virtual intervention
years   tens of years   so long   suddenly on my screen and by her own hand
invisible   inscribing *Green Circle* in the top subject line   using her first her
former original name   the missing person reappears   and will be seen to
   reappear

In praise of quantum physics

I read the book about the cat inside the box
Schrödinger's is the cat's official name   the box is sealed
the cat might be alive or the cat might be already dead
or the cat might be about to die   there is a flask of poison inside the box
and a radioactive source   an atom will disintegrate
the conundrum   how to
know if

where does this world   which is why the book
it is hard to know what will happen when the lid is lifted
from whence we arise   Pandora's box
an apple in the first woman's hand
small birds in the brambles

the cat of course must eat   if it remains alive
the cat will need a bowl of milk
a thought experiment needs no food   but cats

there are apples   milk honey on the other side   but which side
is other   a garden of gadflies   grass   flycatchers   orange fish
in a barrel for twenty-one years   I blame the limits of my knowing
which I have reached   which even Galileo
punishments   pages I've skimmed   the cat   atoms I've never seen
will never see   I blame the church   TV   plastic wrap
I admit there is everything to know and life might be finite
one cat   two birds   enough milk   honey
red apples still on the trees

The table receives her full fury

after Ron Padgett's "The Drink"

I am always impressed when people in films upend a table halfway
through the standard romantic plot. Sometimes in uncontrollable rage;
sometimes from sheer hubris. Everything on the table, half-finished
drinks, olives, crusts of bread, fragments of a marriage crash to the
floor. Then they turn and strut out into the night. Sometimes they are
the hero; sometimes they are somebody's wife. The people at the table,
what's left of it, non-heroes, are understandably uncomfortable, their
laps now so exposed. The hostess places her hand on the sleeve of the
husband's beige jacket and says, *David, you know she didn't mean it.* David
answers, *Yes*, but in an ambiguous tone, the perfect adult response, and
this is how you know this part is only almost real life. In real life, nothing
is perfect, modulated. No one remembers what comment caused the
table to upend like that, what he said to cause Pat's heroic heave. No one
remembers exactly what happened later. We know that she did not set
fire to his car. His car was her car, and she got in and drove home. In real
life the marriage will not last. This is not a true Hollywood movie. This is
just how it was. How Pat told it to me.

•

Suppose upending a table suppose a patio table suppose outrage and a
bottle of wine a varietal of white   Chardonnay suppose Chardonnay
plays a part   take this as development   as character   take this as coming
for years   the age is over thirty   no upending should go unnoticed
upending is always a sign   no absence no absence should go unattended
missing is always missing   take this as a lesson   a sadness   take this as a
life   two lives and missing   mourning   take this as looking for love.

•

Because the moon is round is halved is quartered
crescent   the merest paring still draws the tide from the shore
and gravity uncertainty because
certainly new theories in the air changed me
in a principled and soul-struck kind of way

because the farther back in space we search
the further back in time we see
because my mother was my mother and my father
worked too hard
and my aunt whose name was also Lyda
was a teacher the snowy day she died

because ditches lined the circled street
with culverts under driveways
where one spring the Hurdles' frozen cat
was found stiff as a hard-back book

and language is a ribbon
is braided meteors and shining tails
imploding stars that float the creek
like fairy folk behind our neighbour's house
until one day the creek turned milky white
because fairy queens ruled sea and sky and land
and all the children too   and girls were girls
and flew
and my sister knew four years before
her former lover danced me
through the final days of summer

because Adrienne Rich Nicole Brossard Audre Lorde
wind warnings and weather before the climate changed
I changed
Venus and interstellar nebulae
and so
I fell

in love
with a woman   the way the moon can change
I left my husband   *Leaving Now*   leaving then
not without exquisite sums of all-round family pain
the story could go on
because and so   but no
I fell in love
no tables were upended

I like Pat then and now

I like her now and then I like her then
her ponytail her jutted eyes like fish that sometimes flash
her Morse code her knob of bone of wrist her skeletal self I like her
cautious laugh her haughty shy her simple heaven yon
the way her sister names her then
haughty
and she will not
agreeable as she is
she will not then disagree
and I am not as well unhaughty
then and now though now I try
I try not to be
the word so high and mighty for a civil adult
and she then was just a little haughtier than I which I like
then and now her hair now is white
still so fair   how can that be
these acts of measurement of delicate precision haughty haughtier
these fine-tuned acts of hierarch
multiplicities of childhood rank I like
that then I was not am not the boss the number one big cheese the first
but next in line the eminence
the grisé to her imperial
cartwheels on the grass the world turned on its head now
how can that mystery be
the way she throws a small Indian rubber ball
hard against the red brick wall   calls *stando*
then throws the ball at any moving child I like
her dimple her courage carriage how she holds her shoulders
her chin tucked in and slightly tilted up

the way she hides in the back seat of a car somewhere in my mind
behind a door she hides in trees in ditches culverts
under tables with heavy glass transparent tops
in cities countries tough and down the street
and almost in plain sight

I write in multiverse often but not exactly now inside the Milky Way I want to say the cosmos to say that the girl detective can solve this puzzle in a paperback this crime the way she solves all mysteries between the pages of her multi-authored riddles her flying blue a roadster a James Bond sort of car her father her friends those youthful girls inked inside the pages they know a good clue from a false and crime tape and the place where the other gumshoe drops the notebook in the pocket they find the source before what came before what we could call the smoking gun the Big Bang fingerprints in the multiversatile text eggs before and/ or not before the proud Rhode Island Reds they know girls are links are arm in arm stretching beyond the shining stars which is a form of start a direction out of paper bags the way it works in bungalows and old kitchen clocks not only for girls in detective novels but for all girls with fierce unfluctuating aims.

●

There is a certain wash of light
reveals the cornered fly upon the pane
its filamented feet
its stamped-tin translucent wings   its shine

there is a certain cast of heart
concedes the fly's distress
knows the window's not an openness

and shows the fly egress

The Curve of Time

with arms lifted
—Len Anderson

Fifty years later, how she found me

the technocentric world
the horse the car
we know the thing with silver wings
the radio   TV   in '52 my father bought a six-inch set
Chicago to Dorval   his ears bled on the plane
decompression and the world expands   the binary compels
computers and the cell
though language might obscure
twitter tweet blockchain   a wilderness of speech
and yet
and yet a search   virtual in form   concedes an opening
one day my inbox reads *Green Circle* in the subject line
my first best friend curved back to me in time

One day Pat Hurdle emailed

I awakened this morning having had a dream of you! I usually try to
write down my dreams before doing anything else, like listening to the
news, reading emails which could mess with my memory.

So, I had just written about meeting you in a carefree kind of place with
a group of friends. You were wearing a skirt splashed with vivid colours.
I was telling you how I had tried to Facebook/email you, but it didn't
really matter now as we had connected in person. Then I opened your
email! So strange.

I live in your 'hood. Not quite one house down but pretty close! I've
been here on Linden four years, since my aunt Kitty died. I lived with
her '05–'07, in her last couple of years as she was determined to stay in
her house even after 2 broken hips. She lived to 94. Don't know if you
remember her? She came to look after me, Sue, Liz and my Dad when
my mother was so sick with breast cancer and stayed for 7 years or so ...
returning to Victoria every summer. My sister Sue's family is here. She
died of breast cancer in '98. I was diagnosed a few months later! But still
living to tell the tale.

Yes, let's get together. Would you like to come here for tea one
afternoon, Thursday, Sat? Tuesdays are free for me.

Patricia
Nov. 2011

Before this, she had messaged

I tried sending the following to you via Facebook but never heard back.
Judy McT sent me your email address so I will try again.
Cheers,
P

Greetings dear childhood friend, Arleen, out of the past, fifty some years
or so ago. One of those strange encounters. On a trip east, meeting with
Judy and Barb Palmer for coffee in Dorval, from our Green Circle days,
and they tell me you are living in Victoria and are a writer. I am living in
Victoria too and have had writer's block for the past 3 years. I was telling
Barb, Judy and their mother, Irene, how I remember our childhood
friendship, how we used to walk to school together until one fall you
didn't show up. You were now going to the Catholic school, some kind
of shame associated with this, my feeling of abandonment. Then Judy
tells me the book you've written, Paper Trail, talks about this from your
perspective! So, I found the book at Munro's this past weekend, upon my
return, and have now read it. The thread of your childhood that runs
through it provokes vivid memories, smells of your mother's kitchen, the
countertop by the fridge where your father emptied his pockets. I can see
it in my mind's eye. All this to say hello and invite you to meet for coffee
sometime.

Warm wishes,
Patricia
(I think I was called Patty at age 7, 8, 9)

•

When I first see her after all these years   when I meet her again on her doorstep that day after almost fifty years it is like meeting a mystical being a unicorn or a fairy godmother at the time she does not have a dog nor does she look the way she once looked except for her unworldly blue eyes her hair is white I step inside onto the red Persian carpet.

●

The whole of my childhood the blueprint the imprint the whole silvery lining that foreshadowed my life from then on into infinity is given back to me returned the shape of Pat Hurdle a missing piece puzzlement the first.

•

Meantime, the cosmos. Nancy getting close and closer, backing up into the first two or three minutes. Dead bodies everywhere. False leads. Missing facts. Theories that didn't add up. The Hadron Collider. She ran overlong equations, chalk sluicing down her sleeves.

She could not be stopped. She had already solved the mysterious vanishment of Pat Hurdle, or semi-solved. Pat was found or found herself. Humans are complicated, Nancy liked to say. One alone is enough, but add another, one and one, subtract close to fifty years, and well, you have the start of something that can stir conundrums. Is what she used to say.

Nancy Drew was perfect for The Job, the one who'd find the answer to The Big Old Infamous Unaskable Question, the whodunnit from where whence and how.

Next thing I see on the news, she's boarding a NASA rocket to the past, the first two or three minutes. Nancy could live forever.

•

This means I don't know who she is or how. Past is not the present but is present when the carpet, remaining red, presents itself as red. So much is past. This means the colour, red this, red that, or who I am or was, or who was or who is with me now, it means the colour red remains. This one is who. Or whom. This means the question: which one is past, which one is present: whether she cools with breath or looks, or is it I. Or me. This one is red and velvet and the other, blue-ish silk. Or green with stripes of white. Blue-green is a colour, a pertinent colour, or hue, or whom, but not now with this question hanging and the glamour haunt of grammar, gaunt, going going.

The question is not so much a question as an embarrassment or a scrubbing or a shame, who was left waiting for whom, and on which corner, doorstep, a hard-act-to-follow. Two hands do not make a shake. A question does not mean an answer. This means that two hands might not hold for how long or how intense or how much heat remains after the pie is drawn from the oven. An apple pie. Pie-eyed. Apple of. A sift of heat, a drift, not so much a rift, no, but an inclination.

It means loneliness. It means patience and oversized black acoustic speakers on the wall well before their time and autumnal leaves to wing the wall from outside to the in, crisp red, Day-Glo, branched out above the sofa. The past becomes present and red remains the colour.

New is old with a computer screen inside it, for the virtual, and a blanket and a fox terrier and tea cups and sweet Tulsi rose tea and no oversized speakers. A photograph of two boys in a cuddle huddled. The mother's hair is pale, not because of age, but because of black and white. There is no grey but here.

This means I want to recognize her threshold, her hands, her blue-green fuzzy sweater, the pleasure of her cup and saucer with roses red and yellow a gold rim round and a hairline fracture there, her black shoes, her Irish harp she keeps beside her bed, her bed, her cut roses, pink, her vanilla soap, her back door, her body, face, almost not quite the same. I do not. Entirely. Nonetheless confident. Which I do recognize in her. And her eyes. Not so much her mouth though this does not mean a mistake has been made.

This means windows high off the ground but not high enough to be in the tops of trees. This means a place with a kettle and a quality of light as if winter. A corridor with wood planks polished with a small mat triangularly patterned red, a little green.

A big hole in a life does not mean how it ends, but it is there. The air is slightly off-plumb, gravity problemates, and the door is gravitationally askew. A separation, as if a yawn, does not mean sleep. In two lives, a separation means a question, though one might not mention it. Or more than one. Though one may not mention it, there is still the intention of love.

●

Brash sure maybe crazy to think I could get her back, get back the one who was Queen of the Sky Fairies. Or me back, Queen of Land Fairies, or Sea, depending. Get anything back. One or two mothers. Sisters. Play. A way of life. Not that I would want the whole way. Not the whole way, but maybe the smell of pineapple upside-down cake out of the oven, seven maraschino cherries, one in the centre of each pineapple slice. Or evening in springtime when the light lasts beyond nine, the promise, the wide expanse of sky on those hopeful suburban nights. The smell of new-mown grass. Memory becomes its own ghost orchard.

All her friends now call her Patricia. I find it disorienting; I still call her Pat.

●

Let inquisitive   to be or not or whence
did this is-ness business
start or how   is there a doctor in the house
is there a doctor on the plane or on the boat   let mending start
let being into being   let the doctor though   there is a general sickness
let fishes in their bluish schools
ask and small blue crabs and eels and red plankton ask
and king crabs question shorelines
if only shorelines listened
let questions shift the sands of whatever is still
living   let us live the question according to the poet
if time   then is-ness must   if not real time
let petrels and let glaucous gulls in higher education
let protozoa weigh the scales
let mice and flies and sweet black ants
let air and flume and tea leaves curl
let tarot and names and crystal balls
Einstein   Planck   Feynman and the Pope   let the local grocer
and the baker   books and books and books
let there be an answer   let there be a doctor
in this house of cards

●

Everything else ... is child's play; we must first of all answer the question
—Albert Camus, *The Myth of Sisyphus*

Longing   this absence
of an answer
of any real connection
to the real unsolid past   past the past   before air
before bird
before any thought of bird
is what I have come to understand
is simply life's unsettling condition
of what I am now conditioned to
and yet
and yet the question still has wings

Notes

The opening epigraph is from Anne Simpson's novel *Falling* (McClelland & Stewart, 2008).

Epigraphs for each section come from Len Anderson's poem "The Basic Question" from *Rattle* #49, Fall 2015 ("Tribute to Scientists").

The epigraph for "No question should go unanswered," page 25, comes from C.D. Wright's poem "Scratch Music" from *Further Adventures with You* (Carnegie Mellon University Press, 1986).

The idea for the list of girls' names on page 31 is taken from Alice Oswald's *Memorial* (Faber & Faber, 2012).

The word, "orphine," page 39, was coined by Tanis MacDonald.

The title "Nothing is happening," page 60, is borrowed from Alden Nowlan's "July 15," from *The Collected Poems of Alden Nowlan* (Icehouse Poetry, 2017).

The phrase "ordinary matter" on page 63 is taken from Neil deGrasse Tyson's *Astrophysics for People in a Hurry* (WW Norton, 2017).

Partial found poems, "How Numbers Count" on page 87 and "The elegance of the equation" on page 94, were inspired by Yoko Ogawa's novel *The Housekeeper and the Professor* (Picador, 2009).

"The table receives her full fury" on page 103 is modelled after "The Drink" by Ron Padgett from *Collected Poems* (Coffee House Press, 2013), and several lines are borrowed directly from the poem.

The line "Memory becomes its own ghost orchard" on page 121 is borrowed from Helen Humphreys' *The Ghost Orchard* (HarperCollins, 2017).

Acknowledgements

Pat Hurdle, my first best friend, graciously allowed me to share parts of her life. It is because of her that this is a book at all. So much gratitude for her life, her generosity, and for her friendship.

To the girls of Green Circle, including my own dear sister: I owe you all so much.

John Barton, wonderful poet, read *First* before publication submission, for which I am enormously grateful. Thank you, John.

My two writing groups, as always, offered numerous useful suggestions. Many thanks, to the supportive and talented members of the Fiction Bitches and of the Webbles.

I had the great good fortune to work, once again, with Sue Chenette, brilliant, careful, and very thoughtful editor. Thank you, Sue, for your earlier work on *The Lake of Two Mountains* and for your recent work on *First*.

Much gratitude to the BC Arts Council for their grant funding of this project. Not only did it assist with financial support for the writing of this manuscript, but it also provided reassurance that this collection of poetry was worthwhile.

Finally, so much heartfelt gratitude for Chris Fox, my wife, lifelong companion and first reader, my invaluable and unfailing support and fan.

After many months of illness, Pat Hurdle chose Medical Assistance in Dying. She died on May 7, 2020, on the day of the Full Flower Moon, which was that year a super moon.

Arleen Paré's first book, *Paper Trail*, was nominated for the Dorothy Livesay BC Book Award for Poetry and won the City of Victoria Butler Book Prize in 2008. *Leaving Now*, a mixed-genre novel released in 2012, was highlighted on All Lit Up. *Lake of Two Mountains*, her third book, won the 2014 Governor General's Award for Poetry, was nominated for the Butler Book Prize and won the CBC Bookie Award. Paré's poetry collection, *He Leaves His Face in the Funeral Car*, was a 2015 Victoria Butler Book Prize finalist. *The Girls with Stone Faces*, her fifth book, won the American Golden Crown Award for poetry in 2018. Her sixth book, *Earle Street*, was released in Spring, 2020. She lives in Victoria with her wife of forty years.